# Miss Tammy's Children's Haggadah

Written and Illustrated by

Tammy Kaiser

ISBN:0692685685
ISBN-13:9780692685686

## DEDICATION

To all the families and all the children with whom I have worked throughout the years. Especially to those at Temple B'nai Torah (Bellevue, WA), Kol HaNeshshamah (Seattle, WA), Congregation Albert (Albuquerque, NM), and Temple Beit HaYam (Stuart, FL).


And to Mia, Ian, Max and Toree – my family.

# CONTENTS

# INTRODUCTION

The Passover Seder is a journey through a special meal, just as the Haggadah is the story of the Jewish people's journey to freedom. Seder means order in Hebrew. The meal Jewish families share on the Holiday of Passover (or Pesach) is called a Seder because it follows a particular order. The order in which the blessings are to be said and that foods are to be eaten is contained within the Haggadah. The Hebrew word "Haggadah" means a story or a tale. This Haggadah was written to share the story of an ancient adventure.

This Haggadah was created so everyone can celebrate – regardless of your level of observance, knowledge of Hebrew and Judaism, or family faith tradition and background. Passover is a holiday celebrating freedom, friendship and family.

Follow the steps outlined in this Haggadah for a meaningful and fun family Seder.

# GLOSSARY OF WORDS

**Afikomen** means "that which comes after" or "dessert" and is a half-piece of matzah which is broken in two during the early stages of the Passover Seder and set aside to be eaten as a dessert after the meal.

**Charoset** is a sweet, dark-colored paste made of fruits and nuts eaten at the Passover Seder.

**Haggadah** is the text recited at the Seder on the first nights of Passover, including a narrative of the Exodus. Also, a legend, parable, or anecdote used to illustrate a point.

**Hamotzi** is a blessing recited before eating bread (challah) at the beginning of a meal.

**Hillel Sandwich** is named after its creator, Hillel the Elder who ate the matzah, bitter herbs, and a portion of lamb together in order to fulfill the commandment of keeping Passover.

**Karpas** is one of the traditional rituals in the Passover Seder. It refers to the vegetable, usually parsley or celery, that is dipped in liquid, usually salt water, and eaten.

**Kiddush** literally means, "sanctification," and is a blessing recited over wine or grape juice to sanctify Shabbat and Jewish holidays.

**Maror** refers to the bitter herbs eaten at the Passover Seder in keeping with the biblical commandment "with bitter herbs they shall eat it." (Exodus 12:8).

**Matzah** is an unleavened flatbread that is part of Jewish cuisine and forms an integral element of the Passover festival, during which chametz (leaven and five grains that, per Jewish Law, can be leavened) is forbidden.

**Pesach** is the Hebrew term for the Jewish festival of Passover that honors the story of the exodus of the Jews from Egypt. It begins on the 14th day of Nisan and is celebrated for eight days by Orthodox and Conservative Jews outside of Israel and for seven days by Reform Jews and Jews in Israel.

**Seder** is a Jewish ritual service and ceremonial dinner for the first night or first two nights of Passover. The word is from the Hebrew meaning "order" or "procedure".

---

### The Four Questions Transliteration

Mah nishtana ha'lailah hazeh mikol haleilot?

Sheb'chol haleilot anu och'lin chameitz umatzah,

ha'lailah hazeh kulo matzah.

Sheb'chol haleilot anu och'lin sh'ar y'rakot,

ha'lailah hazeh maror.

Sheb'chol haleilot ein anu matbilin afilu pa'am echat,

ha'lailah hazeh sh'tei f'amim.

Sheb'chol haleilot anu ochlim bein yoshvin uvein m'subin,

ha'lailah hazeh kulanu m'subin.

# 1

## Light the Candles

**As we begin our Seder, we light the holiday candles.**

בָּרוּךְ אַתָּה יְיָ אֱלֹהֵינוּ מֶלֶךְ הָעוֹלָם, אֲשֶׁר
קִדְּשָׁנוּ בְּמִצְוֹתָיו וְצִוָּנוּ לְהַדְלִיק נֵר שֶׁל
(שַׁבָּת וְ **On Friday**) יוֹם טוֹב.

*Baruch atah Adonai Eloheinu Melech ha'olam asher kidshanu b'mitzvotav*
*v'tzivanu l'hadlik ner shel Yom Tov (v'Shabbat on Friday).*

Candle lights
Burning bright
On this joyful
Pesach night

בָּרוּךְ אַתָּה יְיָ אֱלֹהֵינוּ מֶלֶךְ הָעוֹלָם, שֶׁהֶחֱיָנוּ וְקִיְּמָנוּ
וְהִגִּיעָנוּ לַזְּמַן הַזֶּה.

*Baruch atah Adonai, Eloheinu Melech ha'olam, shehechehyanu, v'kiy'manu,*
*v'higianu laz'man hazeh.*

Happy, happy, happy me
To be here today,
And to be Free!

# 2

**Drink the Juice**

The cup of grape juice (or wine) stands for the sweetness and joy of a celebration. We also say a special blessing called the Kiddush.

בָּרוּךְ אַתָּה, יהוה אֱלֹהֵינוּ, מֶלֶךְ הָעוֹלָם,
בּוֹרֵא פְּרִי הַגָּפֶן.

*Baruch Atah Adonai Eloheinu, Melech ha'olam, borei p'ri hagafen.*

Grapes are yummy
Grapes are Sweet
Juice to drink and
Raisins to eat!

# 3

## Wash Your Hands

**Since the next step in the Seder will be the eating of a vegetable dipped in salt water we wash our hands to be clean.**

בָּרוּךְ אַתָּה יְיָ אֱלֹהֵינוּ מֶלֶךְ
הָעוֹלָם אֲשֶׁר קִדְּשָׁנוּ בְּמִצְוֹתָיו,
וְצִוָּנוּ עַל נְטִילַת יָדָיִם.

*Baruch atah Adonai Eloheinu Melech ha'olam asher kidshanu b'mitzvotav v'tzivanu al n'tilat yadayim.*

Wash, wash, wash my hands
As clean as they can be.
Get ready to dip the vegetable
In water so salty!

# 4

## Dip and Eat the Vegetable

We dip a green vegetable (*Karpas*) into salt water and eat it. You can use parsley, celery, lettuce, or any green vegetable that you like to eat. The green reminds us of spring. The salt reminds us of tears. Everyone feels sad sometimes and everyone feels happy. Throughout each year we feel both of these feelings many, many times. In the story of Passover, the Jewish people were sad when they were slaves and made to do hard work. When they were free, they were happy!

בָּרוּךְ אַתָּה יְיָ, אֱלֹהֵינוּ מֶלֶךְ הָעוֹלָם, בּוֹרֵא פְּרִי הָאֲדָמָה.

*Baruch atah Adonai Eloheinu Melech ha'olam borei p'ri ha'adamah.*

Veggies on my Seder plate
Veggies ripe and green
All the veggies that I ate
Reminded me of spring!

# 5

## Break the Matzah and Ask Four Questions

**Take a piece of matzah and break it into two pieces. An adult can hide the bigger piece (called the *Afikomen*) for children to find after the Passover meal.**

**On Passover, we ask Four Questions to explain why this night is different from all other nights.**

מַה נִּשְׁתַּנָה הַלַּיְלָה הַזֶּה מִכָּל הַלֵּילוֹת!

1. Why on all other nights do we eat bread *or* matzah, but tonight we eat only matzah?

שֶׁבְּכָל הַלֵּילוֹת אָנוּ אוֹכְלִין חָמֵץ וּמַצָּה

הַלַּיְלָה הַזֶּה כֻּלּוֹ מַצָּה.

2. Why on all other nights do we eat all kinds of vegetables, but tonight we eat bitter herbs?

שֶׁבְּכָל הַלֵּילוֹת אָנוּ אוֹכְלִין שְׁאָר יְרָקוֹת

הַלַּיְלָה הַזֶּה מָרוֹר.

3. Why on all other nights do we not even dip once, but tonight we dip twice?

שֶׁבְּכָל הַלֵּילוֹת אֵין אָנוּ מַטְבִּילִין אֲפִלוּ פַּעַם אֶחָת

הַלַּיְלָה הַזֶּה שְׁתֵּי פְעָמִים.

4. Why on all other nights do we eat sitting up, but on this night we recline?

שֶׁבְּכָל הַלֵּילוֹת אָנוּ אוֹכְלִין בֵּין יוֹשְׁבִין וּבֵין מְסֻבִּין

הַלַּיְלָה הַזֶּה כֻּלָּנוּ מְסֻבִּין.

# 6

## Tell the Story of Passover

**The Story of Passover answers the four questions we asked. Why is this night different from all other nights?**

**Why on all other nights do we eat bread *or* matzah, but tonight we only eat matzah?**

A long time ago a story was told
about the Jewish people, who were very bold.
They were tired of being bullied, and so they fled.
They didn't even have time to bake their bread.
They put the dough on their backs and ran with their feet.
The sun baked the bread into matzah to eat.

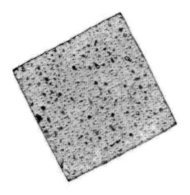

**Why on all other nights do we eat all kinds of vegetables, but tonight we eat bitter herbs?**

During the Seder, we eat something bitter, like horseradish, to remind us of the hard times in our lives and the lives of our ancestors. It is important that we remember all the people who help us be free.

Long ago in a faraway land
There was a desert full of sand
Life was hard and not so sweet
So bitter herbs today we'll eat

**Why on all other nights do we not even dip once, but tonight we dip twice?**

First, we dip bitter herb into salt water to remind us of all the hard work and tears that were shed by those who have helped us be free. Second, we dip bitter herbs into *charoset*, a mush consisting of chopped nuts and wine or juice, to remind us of the mortar that our ancestors used to build buildings and lay the foundation of freedom.

**Why on all other nights do we eat sitting up, but on this night we recline?**

On Passover we celebrate that we are free to lean back and enjoy the meal!

# 7

## Say HaMotzi and Eat Matzah

**First, we wash our hands. Then, we say *hamotzi*, the Jewish blessing before eating bread. On Passover, we eat matzah. Following the *hamotzi*, we say the blessing for eating matzah.**

בָּרוּךְ אַתָּה יְיָ, אֱלֹהֵינוּ מֶלֶךְ הָעוֹלָם,
הַמּוֹצִיא לֶחֶם מִן הָאָרֶץ:

בָּרוּךְ אַתָּה יְיָ, אֱלֹהֵינוּ מֶלֶךְ הָעוֹלָם,
אֲשֶׁר קִדְּשָׁנוּ בְּמִצְוֹתָיו וְצִוָּנוּ עַל אֲכִילַת מַצָּה:

*Baruch atah Adonai, Eloheinu Melech ha'olam Hamotzi lechem min haaretz.*

*Baruch atah Adonai, Eloheinu Melech ha'olam, Asher kidshanu b'mitzvotav, v'tzivanu Al achilat matzah.*

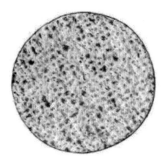

Matzah round or matzah square
Matzah, matzah everywhere!
We say the blessing loud and clear
As we hold the matzah near.

# 8

## Eat the Bitter Herb

**We dip the bitter herb (*maror*) into the charoset. It's fun to make a sandwich with two small pieces of matzah, bitter herb, and charoset. This is called a Hillel Sandwich.**

בָּרוּךְ אַתָּה יְיָ אֱלֹהֵינוּ מֶלֶךְ הָעוֹלָם,
אֲשֶׁר קִדְּשָׁנוּ בְּמִצְוֹתָיו וְצִוָּנוּ עַל אֲכִילַת מָרוֹר׃

*Baruch atah Adonai Eloheinu Melech ha'olam Asher kid'shanu b'mitzvotav v'tzivanu Al achilat maror.*

First I put the apples in
Then I mix in wine
Add a little cinnamon
And nuts to make it mine
Yummy, yummy charoset
It's sticky and it's sweet
Spread on matzah nice and thick
My favorite treat to eat!

# 9

## Serve the Passover Meal

So many things I like to eat

At my Seder table

I lean back and eat and eat

As much as I am able

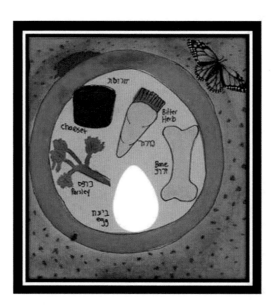

# 10

## Find and Eat the Afikomen

**Adults will hide the *afikomen*, the larger piece of the matzah that was broken at the beginning of the Seder. Now it's time for the children to find the *afikomen* and eat it!**

Where oh where is the afikomen
Where oh where is the afikomen
Where oh where is the afikomen
Oh, where could it be?

If I find the afikomen
If I find the afikomen
If I find the afikomen
I will get a treat!

# ABOUT THE AUTHOR/ILLUSTRATOR

Tammy Kaiser earned her Master of Science in Jewish Education from Spertus Institute (now Spertus Institute of Jewish Learning and Leadership) in Chicago, IL. She has worked at synagogues, a Jewish Federation, and Jewish charitable agencies throughout the United States. Kaiser has two sons and a daughter. She loves to read, write and paint. Kaiser's Doctoral work focuses on Developmentally Appropriate Jewish Education.

The art in this Haggadah was created using mixed media which included construction and watercolor paper, acrylics, watercolors, tempura, collage, colored pencils, markers, crayon, and ink.